This Book
Belongs to

____

Fun Facts

- Cows are known for their gentle nature and strong bond with other cows.

- They can produce over 25 gallons of milk each day.

- Cows have an excellent sense of smell and can detect scents up to 6 miles away.

DID YOU KNOW ?

Follow For Fun & Learn

https://www.youtube.com/@yourartmate

https://www.instagram.com/your_art_mate/

https://www.facebook.com/yourartmate/

https://yourartmate.com

Scan For Similar Books & Fun

Cute Cow in a Field

Fun Facts

- Horses can sleep both standing up and lying down.
- They communicate through facial expressions and body language.
- A horse's ears can rotate 180 degrees to listen in multiple directions.

DID YOU KNOW ?

Happy Horse Galloping

Fun Facts

- Chickens are social animals that love to live in groups.
- They can remember up to 100 different faces, including humans.
- Chickens have a unique way of communicating through a series of clucks and calls.

DID YOU KNOW ?

Smiling Chicken Pecking

Fun Facts

- Goats are known for their excellent balance and love to climb.
- They have rectangular pupils that give them wide vision to spot predators.
- Goats are very curious and enjoy exploring new things.

DID YOU KNOW ?

Goat on a Hill

Fun Facts

- Ducks have waterproof feathers to help them stay dry while swimming.
- They are very social animals and love to be with their flock.
- Ducks can live in both fresh and saltwater environments.

DID YOU KNOW ?

Duck in a Pond

Fun Facts

- Sheep have an incredible memory and can recognize faces for years.
- Their wool grows continuously and needs to be sheared to keep them healthy.
- Sheep are very gentle and love to stay close to their flock.

DID YOU KNOW ?

Sheep Grazing

Fun Facts

- Turkeys can run up to 20 miles per hour when they are in danger.
- Male turkeys are called "toms" and have vibrant plumage.
- Turkeys communicate with over 20 different vocal sounds.

DID YOU KNOW ?

Turkey with Feathers Spread

Fun Facts

- Lambs are baby sheep and love to play and run around.
- They are very affectionate and can bond closely with humans.
- Lambs' wool is softer and finer than adult sheep's wool.

DID YOU KNOW ?

Lamb Frolicking

Fun Facts

- Donkeys have a very strong sense of self-preservation.
- They can live up to 40 years and are incredibly hardy animals.
- Donkeys are known for their long ears, which help keep them cool.

DID YOU KNOW ?

Donkey Braying

Fun Facts

- Hens are very protective of their chicks and will fiercely guard them.
- Baby chicks start communicating with their mother even before hatching.
- Hens can lay more than 300 eggs in a yea

DID YOU KNOW ?

Hen with Chicks

Fun Facts

- Roosters crow to announce their territory and start the day.
- They have sharp eyesight and can see colors better than humans.
- Roosters play an important role in protecting the hens in their flock.

DID YOU KNOW ?

Rooster Crowing

Fun Facts

- Geese are known for their strong family bonds and travel in groups.
- They migrate long distances, flying in a V-formation to save energy.
- Geese are excellent swimmers and can live in a variety of environments.

DID YOU KNOW ?

Goose by the Pond

Fun Facts

- Farmers play a crucial role in taking care of farm animals.
- Feeding times are one of the animals' favorite moments of the day.
- Farmers ensure the animals are healthy and happy on the farm.

DID YOU KNOW ?

Farmer Feeding Animals

Fun Facts

- Barn cats help keep the farm free from pests like mice and rats.
- Cats have excellent night vision, which helps them hunt in the dark.
- Cats love to nap, often sleeping up to 16 hours a day.

DID YOU KNOW ?

Barn Cat

Fun Facts

- Sheepdogs are very intelligent and love to work on farms herding sheep.
- They are known for their incredible stamina and loyalty.
- Sheepdogs can learn to understand many different commands.

DID YOU KNOW ?

Sheepdog Herding

Fun Facts

- Chickens love eating grains, seeds, and insects.
- They scratch the ground with their feet to find food.
- Chickens are great at foraging and can find their own meals if left to roam.

DID YOU KNOW ?

Chickens Pecking Corn

Fun Facts

- Ducklings can swim within hours of hatching.
- They follow their mother closely for warmth and safety.
- Ducklings imprint on the first moving object they see after hatching, usually their mother

DID YOU KNOW ?

Ducklings Following Mother Duck

Fun Facts

- Cows drink up to 50 gallons of water per day.
- They love to socialize while eating or drinking.
- Cows are peaceful animals and enjoy a calm, quiet environment.

DID YOU KNOW ?

Cow Drinking from a Trough

Fun Facts

- Horses love eating hay, especially during the winter when fresh grass is scarce.
- They have very sensitive lips and use them to pick through their food.
- A horse's diet needs to be carefully balanced for their health.

DID YOU KNOW ?

Horse Eating Hay

Fun Facts

- Chicks start pecking their way out of the eggshell before hatching.
- It can take several hours for a chick to fully hatch.
- Once hatched, chicks dry off quickly and are soon ready to explore.

DID YOU KNOW ?

Chick Hatching from Egg

Fun Facts

- Donkeys are incredibly strong and can carry heavy loads.
- They have been used as pack animals for thousands of years.
- Donkeys are patient, but they also have a strong sense of independence.

DID YOU KNOW ?

Donkey Carrying a Load

Fun Facts

- Barn owls are excellent at keeping the farm free of pests like mice.
- They have amazing night vision, making them perfect nighttime hunters.
- Barn owls have a distinctive heart-shaped face and can be recognized by their silent flight.

DID YOU KNOW ?

Barn Owl

Fun Facts

- Windmills have been used on farms to pump water or grind grain.
- Sheep love grazing in wide, open pastures.
- They stay in flocks for safety and companionship.

DID YOU KNOW ?

Sheep and Windmill

Fun Facts

- Geese build their nests on the ground, often near water.
- Both male and female geese take turns guarding the nest.
- Goose eggs are larger than chicken eggs and take longer to hatch.

DID YOU KNOW ?

Goose Nesting

Fun Facts

- Baby goats, called kids, are full of energy and love to jump and play.
- Goats communicate with each other by bleating.
- Kids are very curious and start exploring their surroundings from an early age.

DID YOU KNOW ?

Baby Goat (Kid) Leaping

Fun Facts

- Horses love treats like carrots and apples.
- Carrots are a healthy snack for horses, providing vitamins and nutrients.
- Horses have an excellent sense of smell and can recognize their favorite treats.

DID YOU KNOW ?

Horse with Carrot

Fun Facts

- Hens sit on their eggs to keep them warm until they hatch.
- The process of laying and hatching eggs is called "brooding."
- Hens will often rotate their eggs to ensure even warmth.

DID YOU KNOW ?

Hen on a Nest

Fun Facts

- Calves are baby cows and are often very playful.
- A calf can stand and walk within an hour of being born.
- Cows are very attentive mothers and form strong bonds with their calves.

DID YOU KNOW ?

Cow with a Calf

Fun Facts

- Lambs are born with a natural ability to follow their mothers.

- Mother sheep, or ewes, are very nurturing and protect their lambs.

- Lambs start grazing on grass a few days after birth.

DID YOU KNOW ?

Sheep with Lamb

Fun Facts

- Turkeys can recognize each other by their voices.
- They love foraging for food like insects, seeds, and berries.
- Turkeys are surprisingly fast runners and can fly short distances.

DID YOU KNOW ?

Turkey Walking Through Field

Fun Facts

- Ducklings are excellent swimmers, even when they are very young.
- They are born with a layer of down that keeps them warm.
- Ducklings often ride on their mother's back when they are tired.

DID YOU KNOW ?

Duckling on Lily Pad

Fun Facts

- Cows have been milked by hand or machine for thousands of years.
- Milking provides fresh milk, which can be made into butter, cheese, and yogurt.
- Cows are milked twice a day on most farms.

DID YOU KNOW ?

Farmer Milking a Cow

Fun Facts

- Goats have an efficient digestive system that allows them to eat a wide variety of plants.

- They are natural foragers and prefer browsing over grazing.

- Goats are curious animals and will often nibble on anything they find.

DID YOU KNOW ?

Goat Eating Grass

Fun Facts

- Chickens enjoy roosting on fences or branches at night.
- They have excellent balance and use their toes to grip tightly.
- Roosting helps keep them safe from ground predators.

DID YOU KNOW ?

Chickens on a Fence

Fun Facts

- Farm dogs are trained to protect and herd animals.
- They are very loyal and love helping farmers manage the flock.
- A good farm dog can guide animals with just a few simple commands.

DID YOU KNOW ?

Farm Dog Watching Over

Fun Facts

- A farmyard is a busy place where all kinds of animals live and work together.

- Each animal on the farm plays an important role in keeping it running smoothly.

- Farmers take great care to ensure their animals are healthy and happy.

DID YOU KNOW ?

Barnyard with Animals

Fun Facts

- Horses and riders form strong bonds through training and care.
- Riding helps horses stay active and healthy.
- Horses have been used for transportation and farming for thousands of years.

DID YOU KNOW ?

Horse and Rider

Fun Facts

- Chicken coops provide a safe space for hens to lay their eggs.
- Farmers collect eggs daily to ensure they stay fresh.
- Hens like to return to the same spot in the coop to lay their eggs.

DID YOU KNOW ?

Chicken Coop with Eggs

Fun Facts

- Tractors help farmers plant, plow, and harvest crops.
- Modern tractors are powerful machines that make farming easier.
- Farmers use tractors to transport goods and supplies around the farm.

DID YOU KNOW ?

Farmer on a Tractor

Fun Facts

- Horses need a cozy stable to rest and stay safe from bad weather.
- Stables are also a place where horses can eat and relax.
- A clean and comfortable stable is important for a horse's health.

DID YOU KNOW ?

Horse in a Stable

Fun Facts

- Roosters crow to communicate with their flock and claim their territory.
- They are very protective of the hens and will guard them from threats.
- Roosters are known for their vibrant plumage and bright red combs.

DID YOU KNOW ?

Rooster on Fence Post

Fun Facts

- Hens and ducks can live together peacefully on a farm.
- They often share the same space but have different nesting habits.
- Both hens and ducks are excellent at finding food by scratching and foraging.

DID YOU KNOW ?

Hen and Duck Together

Fun Facts

- Barn owls hunt quietly, making them perfect for keeping the barn free of pests.
- They can fly without making a sound due to their special feathers.
- Barn owls have excellent hearing, which helps them locate prey in the dark.

DID YOU KNOW ?

Barn Owl in Flight

Fun Facts

- Harvesting is an important part of farm life, providing food for animals and people.
- Farmers work long hours during harvest season to gather the crops.
- Crops like corn, wheat, and oats are commonly grown on farms.

DID YOU KNOW ?

Farmers Harvesting Crops

Fun Facts

- Rabbits are common on farms and love nibbling on grass and plants.
- They are very fast and can jump long distances to escape predators.
- Rabbits are most active in the early morning and late afternoon.

DID YOU KNOW ?

Rabbit in the Field

Fun Facts

- Farmers sell their crops and products at local markets.
- Fresh produce like vegetables, fruit, and eggs come straight from the farm.
- Farmer's markets are a great way for people to support local farms.

DID YOU KNOW ?

Farmer's Market Stand

Fun Facts

- Goats are very agile and love to jump and climb on things.
- They have excellent balance and can even climb steep hills and rocks.
- Goats' playful nature makes them fun to watch on a farm.

DID YOU KNOW ?

Goat Jumping on a Log

Fun Facts

- Chickens love scratching in the dirt to find food like worms and seeds.
- They are very social and enjoy being around other chickens.
- Chickens provide eggs and sometimes meat for the farm.

DID YOU KNOW ?

Chickens in a Barnyard

Fun Facts

- Ducks are excellent swimmers, and ducklings follow their mother closely.
- They communicate with soft quacks and whistles.
- Ducks love to forage for food in the water, like insects and plants.

DID YOU KNOW ?

Duck and Ducklings in a Pond

Fun Facts

- Horses are often used for riding and working on farms.
- Saddles help keep the rider balanced and comfortable.
- Horses are strong animals and can travel long distances.

DID YOU KNOW ?

Horse with Saddle

Fun Facts

- **Calves are very playful and full of energy, especially when they are young.**
- **They love running and jumping in the fields with other calves.**
- **Calves grow quickly and become strong farm animals.**

DID YOU KNOW ?

Calf Playing in the Grass

Fun Facts

- Hay bales provide food for farm animals, especially in the winter.
- Farmers use machines to cut, dry, and bundle the hay into bales.
- Hay is stored in barns to keep it dry and fresh

DID YOU KNOW ?

Barn Filled with Hay Bales

Fun Facts

- Horses trust their handlers and are often led around the farm.
- Leading horses helps them stay calm and focused.
- Horses are trained to follow simple commands like walk, stop, and turn.

DID YOU KNOW ?

Farmer Leading a Horse

Fun Facts

- Planting seeds is the first step to growing crops on the farm.
- Farmers carefully tend to the soil to make sure the seeds grow strong.
- Different crops are planted at different times of the year.

DID YOU KNOW ?

Farmer Planting Seeds

Fun Facts

- Roosters crow at sunrise to announce the start of the day.
- They have a special role in guarding the hens and keeping order in the flock.
- Roosters are known for their bright feathers and loud calls.

DID YOU KNOW ?

Rooster and Sunrise

www.ingramcontent.com/pod-product-compliance
Lightning Source LLC
Chambersburg PA
CBHW081256130726
47998CB00010B/2820